HOW TO MAKE

£1,000 PER WEEK

RUNNING YOUR

OWN IMPORT /

EXPORT AGENCY

By Ray Fox, B.SC., FCIS, Principal, The Bottom Line Consultancy

First Edition published in 2015 by The Bottom Line Consultancy

Hurst Cottage, Bottle Square Lane, Radnage,

Buckinghamshire. HP14 4DP, United Kingdom

Tel: 01494 483728 Fax: 01494 484039

Email: fox@estelle-alan.com

ISBN-13: 978-1507722176
ISBN-10: 1507722176

First edition 2015

Printed and bound by Amazon Creates

NOTE: The material contained in this book is set out in good faith for general guidance and no liability can be accepted for loss or expense incurred as a result of relying in particular circumstances on statements made in this book. Laws and regulations are complex and liable to change, and readers should check the current positions with the relevant authorities in their country of origin before making personal arrangements.

This book is available online and at all good bookstores.

BACKGROUND

When you turn the light out to sleep, others, on the other side of the world are just turning on the light and getting ready for work.

Throughout the surface of the Earth, the cycle of production, manufacture, shipment, delivery and then purchase, continues unending. Cars made in Japan are driven in the USA. Dresses made in Hong Kong are worn in the UK. Butter produced in New Zealand is consumed in Germany. Wine made in France is drunk in Ireland. Every minute, every hour, every day, every week and every month of the year, the hustle and bustle of international trade continues, unceasingly.

From your perspective, the interesting aspect of this is that a substantial income can be earned by the application of some fairly simple but established export/import agency trading principles and practices. What is more, the business you are about to set up will be your business. You will own it, you will run it, you will take the profits, you will have the fun ~ what's more, you will have unlimited potential with virtually no risk.

The potential is phenomenal. Let us consider Bill Bloggs. Bill wants to export washing machines to Australia. This manual will explain how Bill will find a manufacturer of washing machines who does not yet have an agent in Australia.

We have included draft outline letters that Bill can use to contact potential manufacturers. We will explain how Bill can negotiate a proper legally binding agreement to be the manufacturer's sole Agent in Australia. We will then show Bill how to find distributors, stockists, importers, and dealers in Australia who want to handle washing machines. Bill's agreement gives him a 12½% commission on every washing machine sold in Australia. In his first year, 100 washing machines are sold at £500 each. Total sales in year 1 are £50,000. His commission, at 12½% equals £6,250. Not bad for starters.

Remember, this is only one product, in one country in Bill's first year. Just imagine what happens next year. The washing machine manufacturer is so pleased, that he appoints Bill his sole agent in New Zealand, Israel and Sweden. In the meantime, Bill negotiates with a French television manufacturer and obtains sole agency rights in Brazil, Peru, Columbia and Argentina. Bill's income begins to increase. However, the exciting aspect of this business, is that Bill's income increases in direct proportion to his effort.

As Bill works harder, his income starts to grow dramatically. What started as a part-time hobby becomes so profitable that he is able to leave his full time job and concentrate on his export/import business. Does it sound appealing? Read on to find out how it is all done.

Contents Page

WHAT IS A COMMISSION AGENT?

A commission agent is not an importer, nor does he export. You will not be travelling up and down the country hawking products from shop to shop. Nor will you be filling your garage or living room full to the brim with imported products that you will then try and sell – unless, of course, you want to!!

Your low-key operation is based primarily on a continuous output of letters, faxes and emails augmented with telephone calls. Our experience has shown that there are literally tens of thousands of companies who want to export but do not know how to do it. They may not have the staff. They may not have the time. More than likely, they have been put off by what appears a far too daunting task.

GOVERNMENT BARRIERS

Unfortunately, there are Government made barriers to international trading. This is accomplished either by a "duty" that is imposed on the imported goods as a tariff or there is a "quota" that restricts the quantity of certain products allowed into the country. These barriers:-

1.   Produce revenue for the Government in the form of taxes.

2. Protect local manufacturers from cheap competition.

3. Increase the price of imported goods to the level of prices of those goods produced domestically so that domestically produced goods are more competitively priced for the home market.

ADVANTAGES OF OPERATING AS A COMMISSION AGENT

Notwithstanding the Governmental barriers imposed, acting as a commission agent has tremendous advantages that are easy to identify:-

1. You are your own boss. You work when you like for as long as you like. During the day, in the evenings, at weekends, in the middle of the night if that is what suits you!!

2. A knowledge of foreign languages is not necessary. English is the international language of trade. English is spoken in the majority of companies in almost every country of the world. Quite simply, language is not a barrier when it comes to international trade, although translation companies can easily be found in your local Yellow Pages, Thomson Directories or on the internet. There are even "do it yourself" translation services available free on Google.

3. You require little or no capital expenditure. A functional lap top or desk top computer, internet access, a printer, a desk, chair, some letter headed paper and a small amount of space and you are in business. This business could easily be run from a garage, a shed, a spare bedroom or even the dining room or kitchen table.

4. The overheads are minimal. This business can easily be run from home. You definitely do not require purpose built offices with 21st Century equipment. When your business grows, you may be inclined to purchase these. At the beginning, your primary expenses are paper, envelopes, broadband internet access, postage plus the occasional telephone call or fax.

5. You do not need any expensive staff to employ. The whole concept behind our system of running an export/import agency is that it can be run by yourself, or, of course, by a couple. But you do not need to employ anybody.

6. You will not need any major capital injection to purchase

stock. You will not be buying or selling on your own account. Your income will be dependant on the goods sold in the territories that you have an agency for ~ but you will not be buying them yourself.

7.   As you will not be buying stock, you will not need a large area for the storage of products. This again, cuts down on the overheads.

8.   You do not need any technical knowledge about the products manufactured by your principals [the company/manufacturer that you represent].   Your role is purely and simply to introduce the buyer to the seller. If you receive any technical questions about the products, these will be referred directly to your principal.

9.   You do not require any specialised marketing experience. As we have said earlier, your role is purely and simply to introduce the buyer to the seller. The seller, [your principal], does the rest.

11

10.   Earnings from the Agency continue for many years. Most of the contracts will be for periods of between five and ten years. Once a relationship has been formed, your income will continue with little or no effort on your part for many years to come.

11.   There is no lack of manufacturers who want you to try and sell their products for them. There is no limit to the numbers of products you may want to handle. There is no limit to the numbers of buyers and sellers. Some agents handle a handful of products in, say, six or eight countries. Others handle twenty or thirty products in just a couple of countries or in one region, say Australia and New Zealand or Scandinavia.

Others handle just one product for a small manufacturer but represent them in every overseas country in the world. You decide. The truly exciting aspect is that new products, new buyers and new manufacturers come into existence every single day. Just go to a local trade show or exhibition and look at all the new products on show. Just see how many buyers there are looking for products to buy.

12. For these reasons, your earning's potential is, virtually, limitless. You can represent as many principals - one, five, fifty, one hundred - as you like. You can similarly represent them in as many countries as your principal(s) wish you to. The only limit is how hard you want to work and how much money you want to make.

13. You will not need a detailed knowledge of Government regulations. These will also be handled by the buyer and the seller.

14. Finally, and perhaps most importantly, the system we have developed allows you to tap in to world's information sources free. In other words, you can let somebody else do the work for you. Governments, Banks, Manufacturers, shipping companies, Embassies, etc. are falling over themselves to increase the flow of international trade. All you have to do is ask the right person the right questions.

STARTING UP IN BUSINESS

Your Office

You do not need expensive or elaborate office space to start up your business. If need be, you could start off by running your business from the kitchen or dining room table.

Your minimal requirement consists of a computer, a printer, internet access, desk and a chair, some filing and shelf space and a telephone/fax. If these are not readily available, the small ads in your local newspaper or a visit to a local boot fair will invariably lead you to some second-hand equipment at reasonable prices.

If you have a spare room, it could easily be converted into an office. If not, perhaps a corner of the garage, bedroom or loft will suffice. Wherever you can work quietly and not be disturbed, nor disturb others, is good enough.

Your trading image

Your image to the trading world, in the first instance at least, depends on what you think of yourself as well as what others think of you. At the beginning, you will be dealing with manufacturers, buyers, etc. who may be on the other side of the world. You are not going to be inviting them into your home so they will not know that your business is being run from, say, the kitchen table. Consequently, you must give them the impression that you are a BIG company and that can only be done by giving the impression that you are a big company. The following will give the people you are dealing with the impression that you are a big company.

[a] Web site and email address

Every big company has a web site and an email address. These provide instant transmission of documents as well as an opportunity to show the world what you can offer. Consider a web site to be your cyber-brochure to the world and for just a few pounds, a domain name can be purchased and a web site set up from companies like uk.godaddy.com or www.1and1.co.uk. In the business world, email is as common as a telephone. Without an email address and web site, you will appear very small and amateurish.

Make sure you show your email address and web site on your letter headed paper and business cards and encourage people to use them as letters from abroad can take weeks to arrive unless couriered.

[b] Professional Qualifications

Some people have been to University and College ~ others have not. Education is not a prerequisite to success in our line of business but your image to the rest of the world will be greatly enhanced if you have letters after your name. Just ask yourself, what is more impressive: Bill Bloggs or Bill Bloggs, M.Bar., M.MAA., M.Inst.SMM., CIF. These "qualifications" (and there are many others) can be obtained by applying for membership of the British Agents Register in Harrogate [01423 560608], The Manufacturers Agents Association in London [020 82534516], The Institute of Sales and Marketing Management in Luton [01582 840001] and The International Society of Financiers, [call the USA, +1.828.393.8908]. When you complete the course with The College of International Trade + Finance, you will be entitled to use the letters, Dip. Int. T.F. after your name.

[c] Professional Organisations

In addition to your professional qualifications, once your business is off and running, you may well consider joining some of the professional organisations such as The Chartered Institute of Management [www.manager.org.uk], The Institute of Directors [www.IOD.com], The Institute of Export [www.export.org.uk], The Federation of Small Businesses [www.fsb.org.uk] and The National Association of the Self Employed [www.nase.org]. You would also be well advised to join your local Chamber of Commerce as other professional business groups in your area as these will widen your sphere of business and professional contacts.

You should also subscribe to *World Money £xchange* [www.WorldMoneyExchange.co.uk] which is one of the main international networking organisations for international trade and finance (01494.483728). As a buyer of this book, you will be entitled to a 50% discount off the annual subscription.

[d] Letter-headed paper

As we have stated previously, your image is what others think of you. Consequently, it is important that you use quality letter headed paper with matching envelopes where possible. As you will send a lot of post overseas, there is always the risk that your mail might go astray. By having your address printed on your envelopes, any mail that is undelivered will be returned to you. In the short term, particularly until your business is profitable, you may consider using a rubber stamp showing your address that you can put on the reverse of your envelopes. A local printer or stationer can do this for under £10. You could also have small labels printed. Try vistaprint.com. These only cost about £5 for 1,000. These printers can also produce a customised logo to appear on your letter-head, business cards and envelopes.

Many small and start up business, use their computers and printers to design their own letter headed paper and then you can scan and email your letters to prospective customers and clients.

[e] Trading Style

Your image improves with a good trading style. Bloggs Import/Export, BB Trading, BB Commercial, Bloggs International Enterprises, Bloggs Global Trading all give the impression of a large organisation. If you wish, you could form yourself into a Limited Company [contact Companies House in Cardiff – www.companieshouse.gov.uk]. You may need to get the advice of a Solicitor and/or an Accountant on the pros and cons of forming a limited company. Whilst on the subject of professional advisers, do not forget to contact your local bank and set up a Business Account, notify your tax office as well as start to keep some form of financial records. Again, any local accountant can advise you here. If you already have a good relationship with your local bank, speak to the Manager - they can normally provide you with a business start-up pack as well as put you in touch with a good local accountant.

[f] Trading Style

If you decide to run your business from your home, you may find it useful to have a business sounding address. Talk to "Your English Office" [go to www.YourEnglishOffice.com. If you are in the USA, try www.YourAmericanOffice.biz. And if you want help answering your telephones (making your business look bigger than what it is), you can get a virtual receptionist from www.VRService.co.uk/boogles.

HOW TO FIND OVERSEAS MANUFACTURERS TO REPRESENT

Millions of companies, in virtually every country of the world, are looking to increase their sales. In fact, it is rare to find a Company that is not trying to increase their sales. Probably 98% of them have no efficient business arrangements for exporting their products to countries that they do not currently export to. But remember, they are all trying to increase their export sales. Your task is [a] locate them, [b] offer your services to represent them, [c] get them to appoint you their agent and then [d] find buyers for their products. Let's start with locating manufacturers.

The greatest asset that an overseas manufacturer has, in general, is their own Government. Virtually every Government wants to increase export sales.

It increases domestic employment and brings foreign currency into the country. Almost every Government produces trade journals, magazines, newsletters, etc. All you need to do is contact that particular Government through their local Embassy or Trade Mission. Every Embassy or Trade Mission for every Government in the world is listed in the London telephone directory and is also available from Google. Just write to the Commercial Counsellor at each Embassy or Trade Mission a letter along the following lines:-

The Commercial Counsellor,

The Transylvanian Embassy [or Trade Mission],

Any Street,

London.

Date

Dear Sirs,

Our Company specialise in importing top quality merchandise into the UK. We are currently handling the following products:-

Perfume

Stainless Steel Cookware

Soft toys for children

Sporting Accessories

We are looking for additional sources of supply and wonder whether there are any manufacturers in your country who would be interested in exporting their products to the UK. We are particularly interested in hearing from manufacturers who do not currently export to the UK.

In addition, we are retained by a number of importers who are looking for innovative consumer products.

Please forward this letter through your normal channels and we look forward to hearing from you.

We thank you in anticipation of your assistance.

Yours faithfully,

Bill Bloggs,

Dip Int. T. F.

Obviously, you will need to customise the letter to suit your own personal style as well as amend it to include the types of products you are particularly interested in handling. However, within a few weeks, you will receive trade directories from all over the world. Do not be surprised if you have over 1,000 names and addresses of manufacturers within one month.

What is more, about 98% of them are waiting for somebody to represent them in the UK. We would suggest that you do not write to every Embassy or Trade Mission right away. Some countries are more responsive than others. Unless there are particular countries that you really want to deal with, perhaps through a family connection, we would suggest you start with Taiwan, Hong Kong, South Korea, South Africa, India and Denmark. These countries will give you a good idea of what to expect and you can move on to other countries when you have more experience.

Once you have received the various Trade Directories, select those products that you consider to be of interest. To each one, write a letter along the following lines:-

The Export Director,
Company Name,
Company Address,
Country.

Date

Dear Sirs,

We have obtained details of your fine products from the Export Trade Directory sent to us by your Embassy in London.

We have considered the nature of your products and feel that we may be able to do business with you on a mutually beneficial basis.

Our Company is a small but rapidly expanding organisation and we have contacts throughout the world with importers, retail outlets, stockists, and distributors.

Subject to negotiation, we would be prepared to represent your Company on a sole agency basis in Great Britain and in any other country that you do not already have representation.
On the assumption that the foregoing is of interest to you, please forward prices for Great Britain and any other countries that are

available and we will forward these to our associates in those countries for their consideration.

Our fees are calculated on a commission basis on all the sales in the countries in which we represent you at a rate and a term of years to be agreed.

Our belief in our continued success stems from the fact that we will obtain profitable business for you in a country that you do not currently sell in. As our commission is based on turnover, if we do not achieve any sales, our services will be completely free.

Please reply by return with your proposals. We look forward to hearing from you.

Yours faithfully,

Bill Bloggs,
Dip. Int. T.F.

THE CONTRACT

Having gone to all the trouble of finding manufacturers to represent, it is now time to cement the relationship between yourself and the Principal.

There are many forms of Agency Agreements and some manufacturers may already have produced their own form of agreement. We have included in the Appendix a Standard Agency Agreement. We have found this document to be sufficient for our purposes in the past. However, we accept no liability for it and if you have any doubt as to whether it will be suitable for your particular purposes, we recommend that you consult your Solicitor.

At this stage, you now represent an overseas manufacturer and have a contract with that manufacturer to market their products in the UK. How do you find UK importers or distributors who would be interested in your overseas products?

The library in your nearest main town or City will contain all the information you need here although a tremendous amount of information is now available from the internet.

Most libraries have the Yellow Pages and Thomson Directories and here you will find the type of outlets you are looking for. Depending on the type of product you are trying to sell, you may want a Department Store, a Pharmacy, a particular type of shop, an importer, a wholesaler, an off-licence, a shop, etc. In fact, if you contact Yellow Pages or Thomson Directories directly, they could even sell you a mailing list with names of the specific types of outlets you are looking for. Other sources would be Dun + Bradstreet in High Wycombe [www.dnb.co.uk] and Experian in Nottingham [www.experian.co.uk]. To each, write as follows:-

The General Manager,
Company Name,
Company Address.

Date

Dear Sir,

We are reliably informed that you are a [stockist/distributor/importer, etc.] who would be quick to seize an opportunity to consider a new line that has not, up until now, been available in the UK.

We represent [Manufacturers name], manufacturers of [type of product]. These products have achieved remarkably high sales volume in [Australia/USA/Canada] and we have been requested by the manufacturer to establish sales outlets in the United Kingdom.

Enclosed is a sales brochure, price list and other details that we are confident you will find of interest. The recommended retail price as shown is not only competitive but will provide you with an exceptional level of profit.

As our Principals are eager to establish early sales networks in the UK, please reply by return indication your interest.

We look forward to hearing from you.

Yours faithfully,

Bill Bloggs,
Dip. Int. T.F.

With a number of minor changes, this letter can also be sent to an overseas distributor or importer interested in products manufactured in the UK or other overseas countries.

The next exercise that you are likely to be interested in, is finding a UK manufacturer looking for overseas outlets.

Unfortunately, there are no Government publications available that list those companies actively looking to increase their export sales. However, Yellow Pages, Kompass Directories [gb.kompass.com], Dun + Bradstreet Directories and many other directories available at your main library will provide lists of manufacturing companies, most of which will be looking to increase their export sales. Perhaps the most exciting way is to visit trade shows and exhibitions and look for products that catch your eye. Obviously Earls Court, Olympia and Wembley in London and the National

Exhibition Centre in Birmingham are the main exhibition venues but exhibitions and trade shows appear throughout the country in every big City. Contact the local exhibition centre and ask to be put on their mailing list and you will receive details of all the forthcoming exhibitions. You can also identify UK manufacturers in newsletters such as *World Money £xchange* who regularly have adverts appearing from UK manufacturers looking to increase their overseas sales.

To each Company who manufacture products that might be of interest to you, write a similarly worded letter to the one above written to overseas manufacturers. You will be amazed to find just how many companies in the UK are looking to increase their export sales and each one is a potential gold mine for you.

Once you have a contract with a UK manufacturer wishing to increase their export sales, you then have to identify overseas buyers for their products.

This is where the UK Government can assist. Very few small and medium sized UK manufacturers make full use of the services offered by the Government. The majority are scared of the bureaucracy and red tape.

Others simply do not have the time, resources and manpower to plough through the vast amount of information available. Using the Government services, you will be able to find the export customers for those manufacturers. Admittedly, you will be using the same services that the manufacturer could have used. The important thing to remember is that they either did not know where to go and if they did know, they did not bother. You know where to go and you have bothered. Consequently, you will be rewarded financially for your efforts.

One of the primary aids to manufacturers looking for overseas markets is The Department of Trade and Industry [www.ukti.gov.uk]. Although based in London, they do have regional offices and you should make the effort to meet with them. Every British Embassy abroad has a Commercial Attaché whose job it is to identify overseas importers, stockists, etc. who are looking to import British goods. These enquiries are all channelled back to The Department of Trade and Industry and are passed on to organisations in the UK who are trying to increase export sales. The Department of Trade and Industry even have "country desks" where you can speak to an individual who specialises in finding potential buyers in each particular country. They can even help you find overseas agents to represent your manufacturer. Another idea would be to contact your local Business Link or Chamber of Commerce.

For example, suppose you have a manufacturer who is prepared to pay you 20% of any sales, say in France. Through the offices of The Department of Trade and Industry, you identify an Agent in France who is prepared to handle the product at a 12½%

commission. If you let him handle all the enquiries, you will make 7½% for doing virtually nothing, apart from finding the Agent in the first place.

The Department of Trade and Industry will also help you with visits to your overseas markets and put you in touch with British overseas trade missions. They also have an extensive library with up to date Yellow Pages, lists of importers, retail shops, etc. from almost every country in the world. You should write direct to them. There are even trade directories published by overseas countries listing the types of products that they actually wish to import. In addition, there are booklets and pamphlets published by the Government's overseas trade missions listing dealers in almost every type of product in the world.

Another useful source of help and assistance are the British Embassies themselves. The addresses of every British Embassy and Consulate can be obtained from the internet. Write to the appropriate Embassy in the country that you are trying to establish an overseas market. Your letter should be in the following format:-

The Commercial Attaché,
The British Embassy [or Consulate/High Commission],
Address.

Date

Dear Sirs,

We represent a British Principal who manufacture the following products:-

Perfume
Stainless Steel cookware
Soft toys for children
Sporting accessories

We are seeking outlets for these products which have already achieved great success in the UK as well as a number of overseas territories.

We shall be grateful if you would forward to us the names and addresses of distributors, importers, retail outlets, stockists etc. who you consider might be interested in carrying these unique British made products.
We thank you in anticipation of any assistance that you are able to offer us.

Yours faithfully,

Bill Bloggs, Dip. Int. T. F.

You will, in about three to four weeks, hear from the Commercial Attaché direct. In some instances, you will receive a list direct from the Embassy. In other cases, the list will be sent to The Department of Trade and Industry and they will forward it on to you. Another possibility is that the appropriate country desk from The Department of Trade and Industry will contact you to offer assistance locally. Once you receive the appropriate names and addresses, you can then get going sending standard letters to each of them sending information and literature.

Another source of excellent information are the banks, both the UK banks and overseas banks. Contact the Banks by letter and ask for assistance. Remember, every manufacturer, importer and exporter has to have a bank. Banks offer many services to their Clients.

When funds are transferred cross-border, Banks make an awful lot of money. Naturally, it is in their interests to increase the amount of international trade as this not only increases their customer's profit but also their own.

So contact UK banks both in the UK and abroad. Contact overseas banks both in the UK and overseas. Tell them exactly what you are looking for, amending the above style of letters to suit your particular requirements. As before, you will be amazed how much help is available completely free of charge.

To a certain extent, the responses you get will depend on the manager of the bank. He may well give you the names of outlets for each type of product. He may help you concentrate on just one product. One point of warning, here. Please let your own Bank

Manager know what you are doing. You may well find that these banks will pass these responses to your own bank to ensure that you are bona fide. This will ensure that your own bank knows what to say to any enquiries he receives.

CEMENTING THE RELATIONSHIP

Having found principals to represent and the potential buyers to buy, make sure you keep your finger on the pulse at all times. Don't just send a list of potential customers to your principal. Keep yourself involved at every stage of the transaction and this will ensure that your commission is paid. Keep in touch with your principal by letter and visits.

Arrange with your principal to forward a copy of every invoice issued to buyers in your territory. You will then be sure of the flow and volume of products and the accuracy of your commission cheques. And believe me, there will be lots of them. Every couple of months, provide your principal with a short summary of your activities, the prospective sales outlets, the likely sales volumes and other matters that may be of interest. However, do not waste their time with unnecessary correspondence, time wasting requests or by trying to over convince them of their wisdom in appointing you as their agent. Once they start to see the sales come in, they will not need any further convincing.

THE SUCCESSFUL RUNNING OF YOUR AGENCY

As with all businesses, there are easy and hard ways of making it successful. The whole point of this book is to teach you what we already know and save you the trouble and expense of making those same mistakes. Running your agency at the beginning may only be part-time when you already have a full-time job. Consequently, time is of the essence so it is best not to waste it.

Writing letters can be a daunting task especially if every one has to be done individually. One way of short-circuiting the typing of letters is to type out a standard letter and then have it printed or photocopied onto your own letter-headed paper. All you will need to do then is to type in a personalised address in the blank spaces. The recipient will never know that you have not sent a personal letter.

If you have the resources, use a small computer and printer. Second-hand machines only cost a couple of hundred pounds and then you have your own word-processing capability. If you cannot afford this, a local word-processing bureau will do this for you for a couple of pence a letter.

It is essential that you keep your filing constantly up to date. You will regularly receive hundreds of pages of information from the various sources and contacts. It is essential that you keep some form of cross-referenced filing system showing principals, importers, distributors, stockists and dealers by country for each product you are handling. Cheap filing cabinets can be obtained from a second-hand office furniture dealer or through the small ads. Another essential requirement is a telephone answering machine. If you are working in a full time job during the day, your calls must be taken. With some answer-phones, it is possible to listen to your messages by ringing from another number.

EXPANDING YOUR BUSINESS

Going full time in your business may have been your original intention right from the start. However, do not let you dream of running your own full-time business become a nightmare that ends up running you.

This is a very important decision and one that you should only take after you have discussed this with your spouse (if applicable), your Accountant and your Lawyer.

As your full-time employment still produces a salary, use the money earned from the agency to modernise your office whilst living on the income of your job. Purchase the necessary time saving equipment that will help make running the agency easier. If you do not need the equipment, put the money you earn from your full-time job into the bank or building society and live only on the money you earn from the agency. After six or nine months, you will see whether your earnings from the agency support you sufficiently. Then, and only then, resign from you full-time job.

APPENDIX

Agency Agreement

This Agency Agreement is made the   day of [month], [year] and is between [name and address of the Principal] of the one part, hereinafter referred to as "the Principal" and [your company name and address] of the other part, hereinafter referred to as "the Agent",

Whereby It Is Agreed as Follows:-

1.   The Principal hereby appoints the Agent as their sole agent in [list of countries where you have sole agency rights] (hereinafter referred to as "the Designated Areas") for the sale of all goods manufactured or dealt with by them for a period of [number of years] and thereafter until the appointment shall be determined by six months notice in writing which may be given by either party after the said period expiring on the 1st day of the month following [date on which the agreement expires].

2.   The Agent shall exercise all reasonable care and skill in the performance of their duties and shall act faithfully on behalf of the Principal. The Principal will do all things reasonably necessary to enable the Agent to earn their due commission

and will supply them with such information as the Agent may reasonably require.

3.   The Agent will forward to the Principal all enquiries they may receive and shall not (without express authority) enter into any contract on behalf of the Principal nor bind them or attempt to bind them in any way, nor shall the Agent (without express authority) receive any cheques or payment on behalf of the Principal.

4.   (a) The Principal will provide the Agent with all necessary samples, catalogues, price lists, and sales literature generally to enable them to conduct the Agency and the Agent shall not be liable for any loss or damage to any such samples or any other of the aforementioned items except where caused or contributed to by the negligence or default of the Agent.

(b) The Principal shall pay all carriage, freight, customs and excise duty, insurance and all other payments reasonably necessary in respect of the said samples and other items, including the cost of delivery to the Agent in the first place and their return to the Principal or as the Principal may order on the termination of this Agency Agreement.

(c) The Agent shall have a lien on any such samples or other items in the Agent's possession in respect of any monies outstanding from the Principal by way of commission or expenses or any other sums due to the Agent from the Principal.

5.   The Principal shall forward all goods that they agree to sell to customers in the Designated Areas direct to such customers together with invoices and other documents in respect of any such sale. The Principal also agrees that at the same time as sending such invoices and documents to customers, duplicate copies shall also be sent to the Agent together with copies of any orders received by customers from the Designated Areas.

6.   (a) The remuneration of the Agent shall be by way of commission and shall be at the rate of [   ] % of the FOB invoice price of all goods sold to customers in the Designated Areas whether from orders received by the Principal through the Agent or by customers direct.

(b) After termination of this Agency Agreement, the Agent shall be entitled to commission at the same rate on all orders accepted from the Designated Areas up to the date of such termination.

(c) The commission shall in all cases be at the said rate on the normal FOB invoice price and no deductions may be made from the commission payable by the Principal to the

Agent in respect of any rebates or concessions granted by the Principal to the customer.

7. The Principal shall pay to the Agent such expenses as are reasonably incurred on behalf of the Principal (or as otherwise agreed upon between the Parties). The Principal shall also pay the cost of all advertising, promotional material, brochures and publicity but no expenses shall be incurred by the Agent without the written consent of the Principal.

8. The Principal shall, on the tenth day of each calendar month, send to the Agent an account showing the particulars of all sales during the preceding calendar month to customers with the Designated Areas together with a statement of the commission due to the Agent and a remittance for the amount of the commission shall accompany the said statement. After termination of the Agency Agreement, the Agent shall be entitled to commission on all orders as set out in Clause 6 hereof and the Principal shall continue to deliver commission accounts accompanied by remittances as above mentioned until all such orders have been executed.

9. (a) The Agent may upon presentation of any account in respect of commission by the Principal, request an extract from the accounts and other books of the Principal relating

to such commission and the Principal shall deliver to the Agent an extract from all such relevant books and accounts.

(b) Where the Principal fails to deliver such an extract or where the accuracy of such an extract is disputed by the Agent, the Agent shall be entitled either personally or through their Accountant or Solicitor acting on the Agent's behalf to inspect the relevant books and accounts of the Principal.

10. The Agent shall not be entitled to commission on the amount of any invoice if such amount shall be wholly or partially lost by reason of the insolvency of the customer. In the event of any commission having been paid in respect of such amount, the same shall be refunded by the Agent to the Principal.

11. (a) In the event of this Agreement lawfully being terminated by the Principal for any reason other than wilful misconduct on the part of the Agency, the Agent shall be entitled to an amount to be paid to them by the Principal by way of compensation for the loss of goodwill and future earnings suffered by the Agent.

(b) Such compensation shall be at a rate of [   ] % on the normal FOB invoice price for all orders supplied to all customers in the Designated Areas for a period of twelve months from the date that this Agency Agreement terminates.

(c) Such compensation shall be payable in accordance with Clause 8 above.

12. Compensation as is contained in Clause 11 above shall also be payable where the Principal sells, leases, hires, mortgages or otherwise disposes of the business or where for any reason the Principal ceases to carry on business or becomes bankrupt or (in the case of a Company) becomes insolvent or goes into liquidation (other than for the purposes of amalgamation or reconstruction).

13. In the event of the Agent retiring or dying, compensation and commission as above shall continue to be payable to the Agent (on retirement) or to the Agent's personal representative (on death).

14. This Agreement shall be construed in all respects in accordance with English Law and for this purpose, both Parties submit themselves to the exclusive jurisdiction of the English Courts.

As witness to this Agreement, both Parties have signed the Agreement as follows:

Signed for and on behalf of The Agent   ....

in the presence of [witness's name]

Witness's signature   ....

Witness's Address and Occupation

....

Signed for and on behalf of The Principal   ....

in the presence of [witness's name]

Witness's signature   ....

Witness's Address and Occupation

....

Please note that export pricing uses different terminology to that in domestic pricing.

The term "Ex-Works" is used to describe the cost of goods literally as they leave the manufacturer's doors. The buyer is responsible for the costs of shipping the goods and insuring them from the manufacturer's factory to the buyer's point of delivery.

The term "FOB" [i.e. Free on Board] is used to describe the cost of goods and includes the cost of insuring them and transporting them to the port of shipment and placing them on board the ship for transport.

The buyer is then responsible for the goods once they are on board the ship, including transport costs, insurance and delivery to the buyer.

The term "CIF" [i.e. Carriage, Insurance and Freight] is used to describe the cost of goods and includes the cost of insurance and shipment to the buyers nearest port. The Buyer is then responsible for the cost of insurance and delivery from their nearest port to their designated point of delivery.

In all of the above scenarios, the buyer is responsible for any local customs and duties. It is possible for the buyer to request the manufacturer to quote an all inclusive price that includes delivery to the buyer's point of receipt. This would then include insurance, freight, transport, shipment, duties, etc. As you can see, this can get very complicated. Consequently, you should establish early contact with a freight and shipping company who can assist both you and your Principals with the proper pricing for such export contracts. Your bank and the shipping company will be able to assist with the export documentation for arranging shipment (such as Bills of Lading) as well as for arranging payment (Letters of Credit, Bills of Exchange, etc.).

It is traditional that commission payments are based on the FOB amounts of export orders.

You will also need to take professional advice as to whether VAT is chargeable on your Principal's export sales.

ABOUT THE AUTHOR
Ray Fox

Ray Fox is sixty one years of age. He originally qualified with a B.Sc. (Hons.) degree in Behavioural Science (specialising in Industrial Psychology and Human Behaviour) from the University of Aston in Birmingham.

After graduation, he studied for and completed the examinations for The Institute of Chartered Secretaries and Administrators. He is a Fellow of the Institute (FCIS). Following that, he studied for and obtained a Diploma in Company Law and a Diploma in Company Secretarial Practice from the School of Accountancy and Business Studies.

For eight and a half years [from 1979 until 1987], Ray was the Company Secretary of a £50m turnover engineering company. In 1987 he joined Dun & Bradstreet, a US$3B turnover company, as their UK Company Secretary. Over the subsequent seven years, he was promoted to Company Secretary of D & B Europe, then the D & B Group and was subsequently appointed as their UK Director of Legal and Pensions Services. He was also Company Secretary of D & B Group's Pension Plan responsible for all administration and £100M of Pension Fund investments. Ray left D & B in 1994 to set up his own Consulting Practice.

For over twenty years, he has been running a very successful marketing consultancy specialising in the Legal profession. To date, he has worked with over 685 Solicitors' Practices, Law Firms, Patent Agents and Licensed Conveyancers, both in the UK and overseas. His support for the Legal profession has tended to fall into one of four broad categories:

1. Helping them generate more Clients

2. Helping them sell, merge or value their Practices

3. Helping them acquire other Practices

4. Helping them with P I insurance and staff recruitment

He has worked for over 300 Solicitors' practices helping them generate more Commercial Clients.

In addition to the above, he is one of the Founder Members and a Director of Core Legal, [see www.CoreLegal.net] which is a networking organisation of professional companies all of whom provide specialist support to the legal profession. He was also a General Commissioner of Taxes and one of the Co-Authors of "Running a Successful Law Firm – Strategies and Tips for Success".

He is active in Freemasonry, having been Worshipful Master of a number of Lodges and is also a member of The Worshipful Company of Chartered Secretaries and Administrators, one of the modern Livery Companies of the City of London.

Ray is also the brains behind a number of highly successful web sites:

www.BottomLineConsultancy.com

www.SolicitorSupermarket.biz

www.RecruitmentForSolicitors.co.uk

www.NEDexchange.co.uk

www.ProfessionalDirectors.co.uk

www.YourEnglishOffice.com

www.YourAmericanOffice.biz

www.TradeAndFinanceDiploma.com

www.StopTheTaxMan.com

www.WorldMoneyExchange.co.uk

www.Estelle-Alan-Group.com

www.EstelleAlanPublications.com

www.CompanyFormationCorporation.com

www.InsuranceForSolicitors.co.uk

www.UKTradeAdvisoryServices.com

www.YourOffshoreBankAccount.biz

OTHER BOOKS BY THE AUTHOR

More Commercial Clients And How To Get Them

A 'How To' Book for Solicitors' Practices
Published: 2014

ISBN: 978-1505488715

I know we don't want to admit it or say the words out loud but here goes – "Generally, Solicitors are crap at marketing". There, I've said it. We all know it's true but what can we do about it? A lot of Solicitors' Practices will spend a lot of money on marketing, but this doesn't often pick up more commercial clients - a group who are often more profitable than a typical private client. This book is about how to get more commercial clients.

Running A Successful Law Firm

Strategies & Tips for Success
Published: 2014
ISBN: 978-1492870890

Corelegal specialise in working with solicitors / lawyers. Between the contributing authors there is over 100 years collective experience. This book aims to bring that knowledge to you – giving you fresh ideas and perspective. Avoid the expensive, painful and time consuming mistakes that most solicitors make and make your law firm a profitable success!

OTHER BOOKS WHICH MIGHT BE OF INTEREST

Constant Cashflow
How to Make Money Flow To You Every Single Day
Published: 2014
ISBN: 978-1 500601225

The problem with 'Cashflow' is that often businesses and individuals are too reliant on just one income stream/ source. Instead of just having 'one/two' jobs or key clients, and 'twenty' expenses, why not turn this around? What this book promotes is that everyday should be a payday - and it explains how and why.

Make The Most of Your Money
How to budget, save and manage your finances.
First Published: 2013
ISBN: 978-1481990639

This book looks at how to make the most of your money. Often the harder you work, the less you have to show for it. This book covers the issue of money. All the stuff you should have been taught in school including income, stocks, bonds, assets, reducing debt, mortgages, loans.

To order further copies of this book please fill in the form:

No. of copies	Title	Price	Total
	More Commercial Clients And How To Get Them	£ 12.50	
	How To Make £1,000 Per Week Running Your Own Import /Export Agency	£10.00	
	For P&P add £2.50 for the first book, £1 for each extra book		
	GRAND TOTAL		£

Name: _____

Address: _____

City: _____ Country: _____

Postcode / Zip: _____

Daytime Tel. No./Email: _____

(in case of query)

I enclose a Cheque made payable to **The Bottom Line Consultancy** for **£** _____

Please return forms to: (Photocopies acceptable)

Direct Mail Dept., The Bottom Line Consultancy, Hurst Cottage, Bottle Square Lane, Radnage, Buckinghamshire. HP14 4DP, UK
Enquiries to: fox@estelle-alan.com

The Bottomline Consultancy (directly or via its agents) may mail, email or phone you about promotions or products. [ ] Tick box if you do not want these from us
www.BottomLineConsultancy.com

www.ingramcontent.com/pod-product-compliance
Lightning Source LLC
Chambersburg PA
CBHW071004180526
45168CB00003B/1280